ABOUT THE AUTHOR

NYANDA FODAY was Birmingham's Young Poet Laureate 2016-2018, and is inspired by the impact that words can have to create, unite, explain and enjoy. She strives to connect with others where she can by sharing and listening to others' work.

All the people I've never been is Nyada's debut poetry pamphlet collection.

All the People I've Never Been

Nyanda Foday

VERVE
POETRY PRESS
BIRMINGHAM

PUBLISHED BY VERVE POETRY PRESS
https://vervepoetrypress.com
mail@vervepoetrypress.com

The right of Nyanda Foday to be identified as author of this work has been asserted in accordance with section 77 of the Copyright, Designs and Patents Act 1988.

FIRST PUBLISHED OCT 2022

Printed and bound in the UK
by Imprint Digital, Exeter

ISBN: 978-1-913917-19-7

CONTENTS

Poet   8

Grow(n) up   9

Answering machine   11

Regret   12

Chimeric   13

Neurotypical   15

Childlike   16

Wounded   17

Realising   19

Forgiving   20

Real   22

Intrusion   23

Butterfly   25

OCD Is So Funny   26

Likeable   27

Introduction to my depression   29

Non dramatic depression poem   31

Work of Art   32

New   34

My head is a very unpleasant place to live
And I've never really felt safe being truly honest about that
But poetry is my safety and my freedom

All the People
I've Never Been

CONTENT WARNINGS:

The poems in this collection come with the following **content warnings**: mental illness, suicidal ideation, a surprising amount of body horror. But all are somewhat softened by metaphor.

Poet

If I was a poet, I could put this into words.
Take a pen to my chest like a scalpel and bleed the feelings out of me
onto paper
And if I was a poet, it would mean something.
I would carve it into quotes for teenagers and their tattoos and their
tumblrs
And they would feel seen
And maybe there is something beautiful in that
And maybe the beauty tastes bitter in a vicious bite of satisfaction
And maybe I would be able to sleep at night
And maybe when I couldn't, I would be a tortured artist,
But when I lie in my bed, the sheets smell unwashed and I am alone
and there are no messages on my phone and it is 4 in the afternoon
and I am rolling over again just so I don't have to be awake anymore-
And maybe if I was a poet, I would be allowed to burn brilliant and
bright and embody life for a short but memorable time,
Instead at the ripe age of 22 I am watching my spark peter out into an
ember that threatens to dull into ash,
Invisible next to an entire world on fire.
If I was a poet, maybe things would be easier.
For me, at least, feelings are much prettier in poetry.

Grow(n) up

They call it growing up.
The process of maturation and adultification
This sensation of ribcages being grabbed and snapped and bent backwards
and outwards
As you realise the security you thought was coming will not.
And the place where they got it wrong was that they thought we were okay,
And that we are now, for the first time, not okay,
When the truth is that we were never okay,
And are now losing hope that we will ever be okay
Because 4 graduates sit around a table and dream of stability and know it is
asking too much
Coughing up over 50 thousand pounds each,
Watching wet spent money that we never touched hit the wood like a
hacked up lung
And we contort backwards on ourselves now
Is this how an adult stands?
And our parents tell us 'Welcome to the real world'
Letting go of our mangled hands
And we send applications to jobs we are overqualified for to pass the days
Knowing that we should not expect anything in return
And adulthood is chasing us down
It is sprinting down my throat
I hold my breath in a last ditch attempt to stop it from reaching my heart-
I am growing up now
Look at my nice house.
I am lonelier than I have ever been.
Fuck.
For the first time there is no graduation in sight and this is the rest of
my life

And I am adrift
And the world is going to shit
I don't know how to hope for a better future-
They called us their future with the same tongues that took our rights away
Laid the trauma deep in the lining of my veins
I bleed defence mechanisms now
Closed off and cut off
And they say that your twenties are a time to cut loose
But we can't
We grew up too soon / We haven't grown up enough yet
There was some complication in the process
Something delicate was crushed when it was still unborn and developing
I should have been protected
I wish I had been protected
Yes I am a snowflake and I am melting like all the others
And the water levels have been rising for so long
I was never going to be anything more than a flood of emotion
All I do is lie in my bed and drown.
And I can fucking hear those words
Tongues lashing them into my skin
Dismissive and mocking

Answering machine

Most days I feel like an answering machine
Just a record of the things people said to me

"Are you okay?"
The number you have called is fine
"Do you want to meet up?"
The number you have called is too tired
"You would say something if it was really bad right?"
Please leave your message after the beep
    I throw my phone across the room and go back to bed
Sorry the number you have called is busy, please leave a message and a carefully
crafted representative will get back to you
Reassure you
The number you have called is fine
I have *no – new – messages*
I have *too – many – messages*

I become a record of everyone else's thoughts
Fall asleep to the soothing lull of
The number you have called is busy, please leave a message after the tone

Regret

Regret has taken my body so many times that I now leave a key under the doormat in the hopes that this time it will not break a window to get in.
Leave me shattered and broken
I am hospitable in the hopes it does not surge through me so angrily,
It is angry anyway
That is its nature.
It beats and burns me,
Leaves tears down my arteries to watch me bleed from the inside out
Better out than in.
It leaves me lungs heaving,
Broken on the bed
It is not considerate enough to cover me
I am bared to anyone who could see me
I keep my door locked now
Stuff clothing down over my mouth to hide the violent expulsion of everything regret forced down my throat,

This is what's left when regret takes my body:

Fragile bird bone breakages down my spine
I might as well be spineless now
So I fold in on myself
Contort limbs into woven threads and hold myself together,
And I mend,
I become patchwork skin
Find the strength to stand up as regret slips back in.

Chimeric

Some days I try to trace slavery in my skin.
I look for the seam that splits me down the middle-
It is inevitable
My father grew up in a country that sat on the gold coast,
My mother grew up as Cambridge graduate and Judge's daughter-
I look for the seam more frantically,
Run fingernails across skin in the hopes of feeling it catch,
Some days I want to unpick it
To unravel the ties,
The crossed lines
To find something simpler to solve/
To pick a side
Once and for all.
I am at my limit,
Confused about where I exist,
In the social cawing of binary arguments I am left strung and
stretched between two monoliths
I imagine it like mitosis.
Like one night when I go to bed I might just split and wake up as a
white girl and a black girl and we would just stare at each other:
Oppressed and oppressor
And black me would hit white me and white me would let her.
Black me would apply for bursaries and positive discrimination
minority seeking capitalist performative diversity jobs
White me would stumble wide-eyed through connections and
dinner parties
With grandparents' friends who have an in-
White me would take my share of my great great aunt's inheritance.

White me would post black squares and black me would post stories about white people like white me
And both would turn to their respective communities.
Both would know clearly when they were being spoken to
White me would read the books on the influencers' lists and black me would live the stories in them
Black me would learn about her culture and make black friends and white me wouldn't notice that every room she walks into is white.
White me would send black me well-meaning DMs when there's been another death and black me would have to educate her.

Things would be a lot clearer.

But I do not have a seam.
And multicellular organism duplication through a single round of mitosis is a sin against biology,
So I am just me.
Holding both halves inside my skin accounting for the fact that they do not fit together so nicely
Recognising that I am not half and half, but another thing entirely
And that is okay, most days.
But on the some days
When my skin is taut
And I feel ghost needles darting in and out, all over,
There is nothing I can do but write poetry

Neurotypical

I ask the version of me that was never going to be mentally ill how
many times her brain hurt her today.
She steps back, face twisting in fear from my unstable form getting
closer
Like I'm going to climb into her skull
Like I'm going to absorb whatever neurotypical magic happens
there,
I ask her: How many times today have you imagined the break of
your collarbone beneath the palm of your hand?
  Did it hurt and if it didn't did you wish it did
  Did you imagine a thumb and forefinger slip to ring a ring a
roses around the bone,
  Because in your head, your fingers glide through your flesh
like it's butter?
She takes another step back
I press closer
Mouth twisted in a fake moan of fake pleasure, I ask her:
  How many times today have you felt primal raw panic
licking its way down your veins as you lie still in a bed, still lying to
yourself, still wondering why you don't get better
  Asking yourself if this is what you like,
  If you've grown addicted to the rush of helplessness and the
reassurance that you are
   In fact
   Not okay?
She runs away.
I let her escape
I watch her go.
Swallow down the taste of blood in my mouth

Childlike

I am all spilt milk and apologies
My seams unravelled to threads,
Like a poster for personal destruction, I implode
Intimately
Let myself shatter across the page and freeze the pain and display it
to anyone who wants to see:
This is the art of my loneliness
My heart
My brokenness
It is handmade
It is made out of dry pasta and glue
Like I am a child
This isn't how I imagined it would be.
This is my artwork.
It is sloppy, needs improvement, and I will spend 5 minutes arguing
with Mr Bassett about why I prefer it in monochrome.
Sometimes I don't know how to engage in colours.
Sometimes colours distract me from form.
And he will tell me that something is missing and I will tell him that
that is the point.
I stick down another piece of penne.
There's no point in crying over it.

Wounded

Some days I feel like an open wound.
Lying here, bleeding out for all to see.
Luckily I am the only one around
So I can take the time.
Let the bleeding stop.
Stitch myself up.
Apply dressings and medical tape and wait.
Change them daily and choose not to be alarmed when it is taking
too long
I stop caring quite so much
I trust that it will fix itself, as it always has
No one else needs to know because it will either be fine or it won't
I don't seem to have a strong response whichever way it might go-
So it probably doesn't matter.
I'm just lying here.
Ignoring whatever insides might be seeping out and soaking in-
It is disgusting.
And I should probably change these sheets.
But I won't,
Not for a while
Because it doesn't seem worth it when I know I will bleed again, not
long from now
And as long as no one else knows
-And I don't see how they could
It doesn't matter.
I can live with this
Life is messy
And the bumps and bruises along the way prove we are alive

And they show us that we can heal,
And the scars remind us that we can't heal everything.
And the stressed peeling skin reminds me that I am temporary and
frankly I like it better that way
I tear a bit that is annoying me with my teeth
It feels feral but necessary
I bleed.
I can lie here, just a while
Let the open wound take its time to right itself
And no one else needs to know,
This is just the way of things,
We bleed most comfortably on our own.

Realising

It is the burn of stomach acid that you swallow back down
A balloon with a pin pressed just lightly enough that it isn't quite
bursting

I spot my own emotions like a shape in the distance
I am my own bogeyman

It is looking back and feeling like a child that has been playing dress
up all this time
Wondering who was watching me trip over hems in too big boots

The words taste sour

I keep them anyway

Forgiving

I am learning to hold my pain and my love in both hands.
Trace scars of missteps and mistakes, and words that stayed far
longer than the person who said them ever meant them.
I have an obsession.
A neurodivergent need to pick apart the pieces of me and hold them
to the light to see what trauma shines through the paper-thin
receipts I have collected over the years.
People are people.
The people who loved me may not have known how best to love me
And the people who know you best will always best know how to
hurt you
Both are true:
1. They didn't mean to
2. They still hurt you
Intention and consequence are toxic lovers.
And now, you are drifting away from me again
I don't know if you expect me to jump in and swim after you, but I
have been drowning for too long all on my own so I won't.
I won't.
And I don't care that I care, and I don't care that it hurts
I have learned
People are people
They will always be fallible.
And if you love someone you have to let them go-
That's not what this is,
This is me loving you enough to let you do what you need to.
This is also me choosing not to tear myself apart to stick you back
together again-

This is me choosing to be selfish,
I am not the person you had hoped I'd be
I have learned more than subservience
I choose myself-
Because if you get to then so do I.
This is me saying goodbye.
Not because I never want to see you again but because I never want
to have to hope to see you again
This is how I choose to not be let down by you-
If you love someone, you have to let them go
And if you're waiting for them to come back then they're never
really gone
And maybe you never really loved them-
I am choosing to not hurt myself with you anymore.
It's a kindness I'm not sure you deserve,
But I'm not sure that kindness needs to be deserved to be given so
have it anyway.
I am learning to hold the love that you gave me and the pain you
have caused me in both hands.
But I will do that without you.

~~Forgiving 2.0~~ To My Father

You didn't deserve my forgiveness
You don't deserve my grace

Real

"I barely even exist today" they think
She touches its cheek
His head
Her chest.
Crawls under their covers
Disappears into the darkness behind her eyelids
He is as quiet and small as they can twist her body into being
It erases all tangible evidence that she is here
I am reduced to a silent, still lump
You could not hear their breaths if you tried

Intrusion

There is an incision waiting in my chest
I can feel it
It moves vertically down my body
Between my breasts
There is a satisfaction to be found in the symmetry
That's supposed to be a thing
-For people with OCD
The incision is throbbing
Red hot intrusive thought
Phantom versions of my hands reach in
And I can hear the snap of bone.
This one is a clean break.
Surgical in precision.
We must excise the rotting flesh and I suspect the very core of me is
beyond saving
So reach in to red and wet
Perhaps this is the truest way I can hold myself
(My non-phantom hands are wrapped around my chest)
I can feel organs between my fingers
This is the tactile cousin to double vision and sensation blurs in a
heady beat,
Phantom fingers squeeze,
I am slowly rifling through my phantom body
For me, intrusion is a thin overlay of existence,
Like my life has been taped over by something transparent,
Or perhaps it is more like invisible ultraviolet markings on petals,
No one else sees the frequencies my brain uses to play out these
fantasies

And I am left feeling in technicolour on an over-saturated screen
I'm sorry that I get overwhelmed so easily
I don't work like you do and I cannot work like you do
I have tried.
These thoughts are not mine in the same way that numbers in the
news are not people:
Reality rejected out of necessity
To keep coping,
To move on with your day.
The incision fades.
Sinks back down into flesh and once more, skin is just skin
And the only hands I have are the ones that touch real things,
And my organs return to incomprehensible certainties of un-sense-
able presence.
I will stay whole tonight

Butterfly

Sometimes when a feeling becomes too much I tuck it away in between my ribs,
Leave edges sharp enough to dig in when I wind my spine too tightly-
It's important that I am reminded that someone still lives here in my body.
My ribcage has become ornate with paper decorations that pierce through my skin
Ripped edges of loneliness line my waist to accentuate my hourglass shape,
One day a strong enough wind will catch and carry me away,
Perhaps this is my metamorphosis
And the space between bedsheet and duvet is just a soft sort of chrysalis,
I'm becoming an adult now.
Whatever that means.
I will leave shed skin and compacting coping mechanisms behind me,
I am building my wings out of the very things that were too much for me to hold,
I will explode out of this stale stage of life
And I will rise up into something better.
Leave all my scars on display and shift and twist them into works of art along my skin
I will begin
Finally finally
Something new for me.
The next tomorrow will be better.
It has to be

OCD Is So Funny

When I open the door

And she trots into view

I stand in the doorway
And cry

She is alive
She is alive
She is alive

Likeable

I told myself that I stopped trying to fit a long time ago
I tell other people that too.
The truth is
There is still a second of realisation every time I look in a mirror
Or a group picture.
A reminder.
The me in my head doesn't match the one in my skin-
That complicates things.
You have to go back to the basics,
Every week you relive your identity crisis
In this time of self-definition and ownership I'm collecting labels like
I do insecurities
It is a fun, obsessive hobby
I carve them into the very core of me with eyeliner and poetry
I am very niche.
That's a nice way of saying annoying,
Or overwhelming,
Or there's just something not clicking-
I'm a loud introvert
Which doesn't make a lot of sense,
And the way that I cling to my friends like safety nets might lead you
to mistake me for a people person
It's a contradiction,
I tend towards contradictory
There are a lot of difficult pills to swallow
So you have to build up a tolerance,
Mine is a special type of toxicity
It comes from an awkward need to please,

A touch-starved craving of contact paired with uncomfortable
hyperawareness of skin on skin-
It's not that I'm trying to fit in
I promise I learned a long time ago that people like me are not easy
to know very deeply
And I have stopped slicing off the excess that spills over the clearly
marked boundaries,
The struggle comes in the moments between-
When it becomes very easy to forget that I am not the me that I
imagine myself to be.
It is in those moments that I find myself retracing the irregular
shapes of my personality,
Still unable to commit them to memory.

Introduction to my depression

This is my depression.
I describe her in poems about drowning where she is deep and blue
and beautiful in a cinematic and tragic sort of way.
She holds me suspended
Envelops me
The embrace of a lover who cannot bear to be alone,
Is willing to kill, if only because a corpse can't swim away.
Some days we do battle
And she is a storm
She is a firm hand on my scalp pushing me under
A wave filling my mouth with every gasp that I take
And I am a thrashing thing
Eyes wide
And violent
Resisting
Determined to keep breathing
Believing that I might still find a boat or driftwood or something
Lungs burning
Still fighting.

On the gentler days,
We entwine our legs lazily.
She runs her hands up and down my arms, and I let her
She pulls me back under the covers
The sea is still and I am deep and my eyes are closed,
I look like a moment from a film:
Rippling light filters down to illuminate my hair as it drifts around
my face and it is impossible to tell if I am sinking or rising

So I give in-
It is a much easier day to live.

Ever since I was little I have always loved the sea,
My mother named me her water baby,
To this day I can spend hours alone in the waves
There is an undeniable poetry in the idea of returning to the ocean.

In the shower, I cup my hands beneath my chin to let the water pool up
over my mouth and nose and eyes
An artificial submersion.

This is my depression.
She is as many things as the sea is
And perhaps it is because of her that I watch the moon so carefully
And perhaps it is because of her that I have always found comfort in
gentle rocking- rhythmic and repetitive motion is an integral part of me.

This is my depression
    And I am not allowed to love her
        And I am not allowed to hate her
            So I do both, intimately.

I hold her beneath my skin.
If I could choose another life,
I would not have her,
And in that life, I would not be me,
But she can't be angry-
After all, it is her very presence that makes any sort of death
so appealing

Non dramatic depression poem

The clouds have been painted a light grey
Leaving the sun a white thumb smudge I still can't quite look at
But the grass is still the same vivid green
And the random wild daffodils are just as yellow as the carefully
planted ones
And my dog's nose is eagerly to the wind
And she doesn't notice
So I let the sky cry for me

Work of Art

Sometimes, when I am feeling a special blend of sad and sexy and
lonely,
Like the subject of a painting that did not make the display,
I mentally trace rivers down my spine.
I am always lying down. I am topless right now.
It's all about being provocative in the most sterile sort of way.
And I can feel the wayward brushstrokes of the flyaway curly hairs
that a modern photo editor would erase,
And my face
Would be rounded and smoothed out, in texture and tone,
Warm colours in the background,
The yellows and browns that seem to haunt so many of the famous
old paintings.
I am too often too indoors for greenery and scenery
I am something far more static you see
So I give myself over to the concept of still life,
I embody statuesque
As my body metamorphoses into Rubenesque
And my nipples turn tasteful under the watchful eye of social media
algorithms
And a British man from the museum is coming to cut off my nose to
make me more believably caucasian
My bed is my chosen platform.
The visitors will swear that my phone camera seems to point at them
wherever they go ,
And a legend will rise up that a single touch to my cold, unyielding
skin will bring good luck
And greasy living hands will rub away at my marble and/or paint

I will crumble until someone in restoration comes to pay gentle and close attention to my form,
But they will be careful to only do that which can be undone,
And I will be returned to the back room and forgotten,
Slowly slough off the excess
Till all that is left is the winding shape of my fluvial spine,
Casting rippling shadows when it is hit by the right light,
It is a fine and beautiful way to die

New

Peel back the layers
Let the new skin emerge
Find its place
Grow
Scrub away dirt and scars
Yesterday's lack of sleep and last week's deadlines
Shed
Moult until you are soft and vulnerable
Easily broken
This is a new beginning
Somewhere beyond all and any past mistakes
Break
Break again
Keep doing it if only to prove that you can
Heal aggressively
Determinedly
Like it's a choice
Own your body
Like you have a choice
Loop a small tag in the buttonholes of your new skin
On that, engrave your name
Your face
Your home
This is yours now.

ABOUT VERVE POETRY PRESS

Verve Poetry Press is a quite new and already award-winning press that focussed initially on meeting a local need in Birmingham - a need for the vibrant poetry scene here in Brum to find a way to present itself to the poetry world via publication. Co-founded by Stuart Bartholomew and Amerah Saleh, it now publishes poets from all corners of the UK and beyond - poets that speak to the city's varied and energetic qualities and will contribute to its many poetic stories.

Added to this is a colourful pamphlet series, many featuring poets who have performed at our sister festival - and a poetry show series which captures the magic of longer poetry performance pieces by festival alumni such as Polarbear, Matt Abbott and Genevieve Carver.

The press has been voted Most Innovative Publisher at the Saboteur Awards, and has won the Publisher's Award for Poetry Pamphlets at the Michael Marks Awards.

Like the festival, we strive to think about poetry in inclusive ways and embrace the multiplicity of approaches towards this glorious art.

https://vervepoetrypress.com
@VervePoetryPres
mail@vervepoetrypress.com